curious about

HURRICANES

BY RACHEL GRACK

AMICUS LEARNING

What are you

curious about?

3
CHAPTER THREE

Stay or Go

PAGE
18

Curious About is published by
Amicus Learning, an imprint of Amicus
P.O. Box 227, Mankato, MN 56002
www.amicuspublishing.us

Editor: Ana Brauer
Series Designer: Kathleen Petelinsek
Book Designer and Photo Researcher: Kathleen Petelinsek

Library of Congress Cataloging-in-Publication Data
Names: Koestler-Grack, Rachel A., 1973– author
Title: Curious about hurricanes / by Rachel Grack.
Description: Mankato, MN : Amicus Learning, an imprint of Amicus, [2026] | Series: Curious about extreme weather | Includes bibliographical references and index. | Audience: Ages 6–9 | Audience: Grades 2–3 | Summary: "Where do hurricanes happen? Learn the causes and effects of one of nature's most powerful weather events in this question-and-answer book for elementary-aged readers. Includes infographics, table of contents, glossary, books and websites for further research, and index"— Provided by publisher.
Identifiers: LCCN 2025012823 (print) | LCCN 2025012824 (ebook) | ISBN 9798892008402 library binding | ISBN 9798892009065 paperback | ISBN 9798892009720 ebook
Subjects: LCSH: Hurricanes—Juvenile literature
Classification: LCC QC944.2 .K68 2026 (print) | LCC QC944.2 (ebook) | DDC 551.22—dc23/eng/20250717
LC record available at https://lccn.loc.gov/2025012823
LC ebook record available at https://lccn.loc.gov/2025012824

Photo Credits: Alamy Stock Photo/Peter Brogden, 2, 12; Shutterstock/Arthur Villator, 2, 5, BEST-BACKGROUNDS, 9, BlueRingMedia, 10–11, Captainz, 13, David Pereiras, 19, Dmytro Gilitukha, 20–21, flashpict, cover, 1, Gregory Simpson, 14–15, tonyz20, 3, 18; Wikimedia Commons/ Elliott, William, Lt, 17 (bottom), Walter Hellebrand, 17 (top)

CHAPTER ONE

What are hurricanes?

They are giant **tropical** storms. They start over the ocean. Some strike land with wild force. Heavy rains hammer down. Terrible winds uproot trees and rip apart houses. Waves as tall as buildings pound the coastline. Take cover! Hurricanes are one of the largest and most powerful storms of nature.

Hurricanes often flood beaches and towns near the ocean.

Where do hurricanes happen?

This map shows where hurricanes, typhoons, and cyclones form and where they go.

They form over warm oceans around the world. Nearby coasts face danger. Since 2016, the US Gulf Coast has had one almost every year. Some also hit the East Coast and Hawaii. They are called cyclones and typhoons in other parts of the world.

OCEAN STORMS
TROPICAL DEPRESSION 0–38 mph (0–61 km/h)
TROPICAL STORM 39–73 mph (62–117 km/h)
HURRICANE, CYCLONE, OR TYPHOON 74 mph (119 km/h) and above

How often do they strike?

Nearly 100 tropical storms build over oceans every year. About half become hurricanes. Not all hit land. Only two or three might strike North America. They are most likely during hurricane season. This runs from May to November.

DID YOU KNOW?
2005 set the US record for most hurricanes with 15.

A hurricane swirls over the East Coast of the United States.

How does a hurricane form?

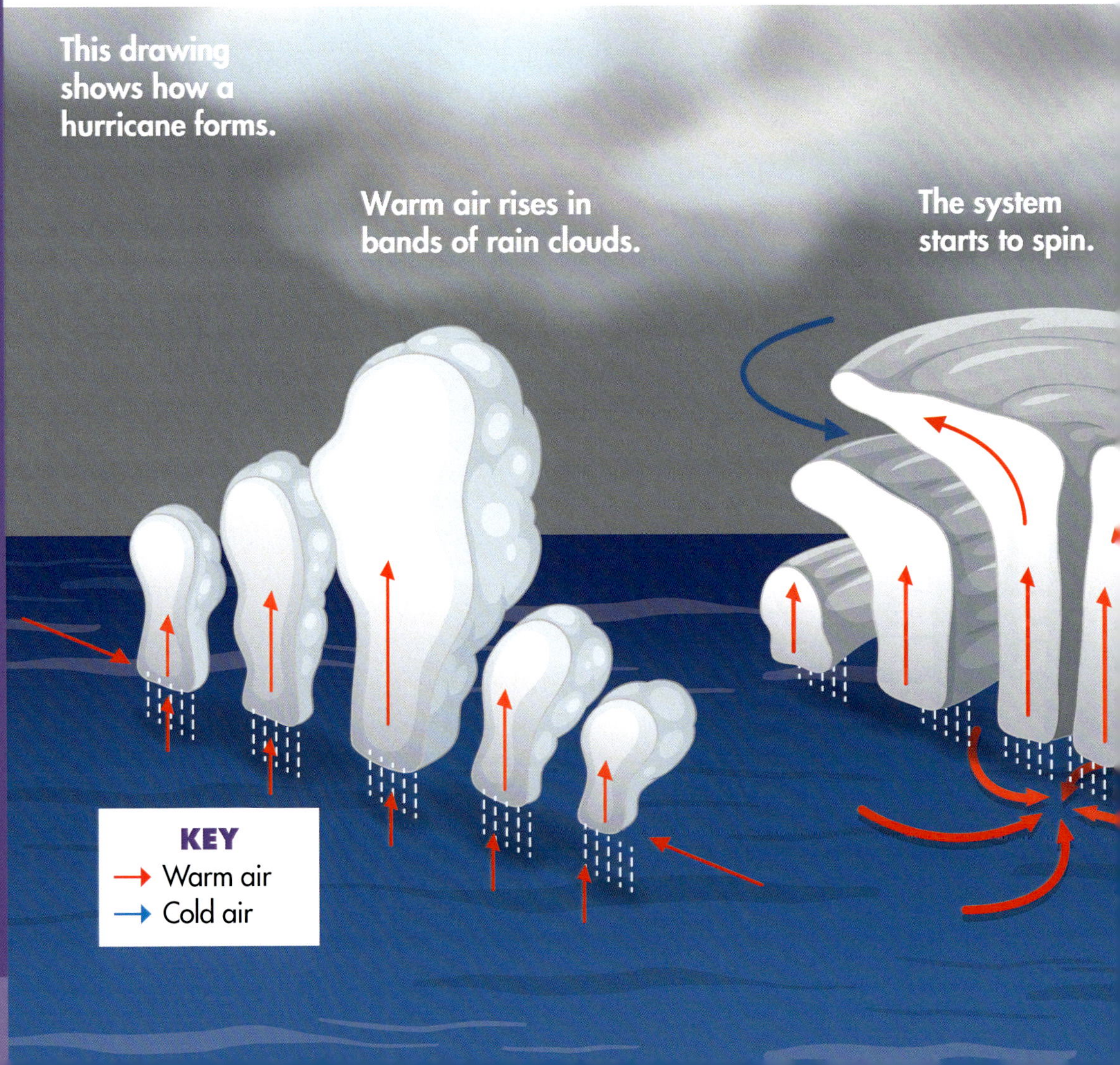

This drawing shows how a hurricane forms.

It begins with a band of rain clouds. Warm ocean air rises into the storm system. It cools and turns into water droplets. More warm air rushes upward. The system starts to spin. An **eye** forms in the center. It sucks up more ocean heat. The storm grows larger and spins faster.

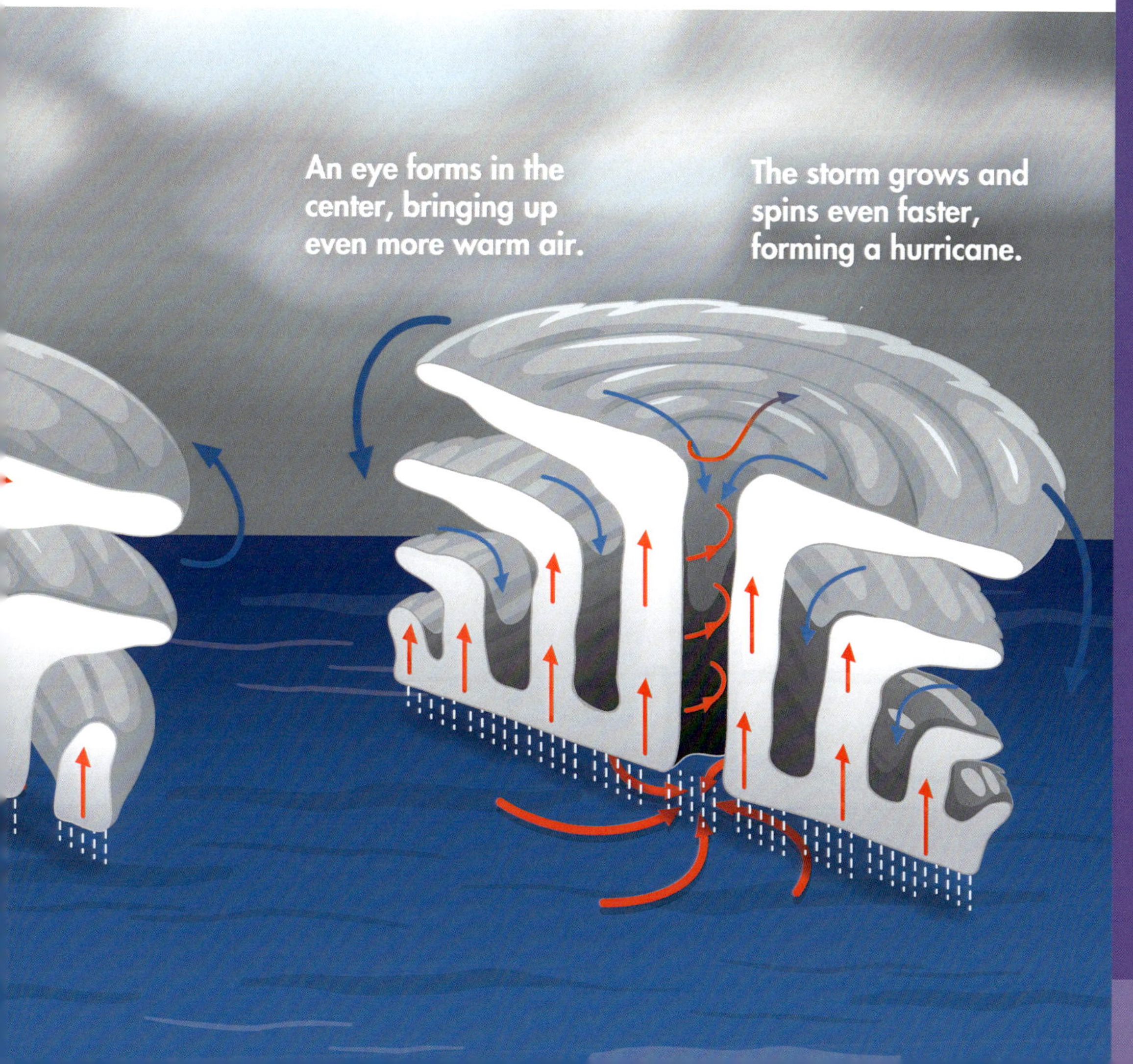

How strong do hurricanes get?

Some storm hunters fly planes into big storms to learn about them.

They are rated by wind speed. There are five categories. Even weak storms can snap trees and **damage** houses. The strongest storms blow more than 155 miles (250 km) per hour! They bring **storm surges** 18 feet (5.5 m) tall. These wipe out buildings and flood whole cities.

CATEGORY 1

Wind: 74–95 mph (119–153 km/h)
Storm surge: 4–5 feet (1.2–1.5 meters)
Damage: light

CATEGORY 2

Wind: 96–110 mph (154–177 km/h)
Storm surge: 6–8 ft (1.8 to 2.5 m)
Damage: moderate

CATEGORY 3

Wind: 111–130 mph (178–209 km/h)
Storm surge: 9–12 ft (2.6–3.9 m)
Damage: extensive

CATEGORY 4

Wind: 131–155 mph (209–250 km/h)
Storm surge: 13–18 feet (4–5.5 m)
Damage: extreme

CATEGORY 5

Wind: over 155 mph (250 km/h)
Storm surge: over 18 ft (5.5 m)
Damage: catastrophic

Why do hurricanes have names?

In 2005, Hurricane Katrina damaged homes, roads, and buildings in Louisiana.

DEADLIEST ATLANTIC NAMES

HURRICANE MITCH
YEAR: 1998
CATEGORY 5
OVER 11,000 DEATHS

HURRICANE MARIA
YEAR: 2017
CATEGORY 5
2,975 DEATHS

Good question! Many ocean storms often happen at once. All storms get named. This helps us keep track of them. Each ocean has lists of male and female names. They go in alphabetical order. Names of very deadly or costly storms are never used again.

HURRICANE KATRINA	HURRICANE GILBERT	HURRICANE CAMILLE
YEAR: 2005	YEAR: 1988	YEAR: 1969
CATEGORY 5	CATEGORY 5	CATEGORY 5
1,833 DEATHS	318 DEATHS	256 DEATHS

What was the worst hurricane in the world?

It struck the Caribbean Islands in 1780. This was during the Revolutionary War. No one could measure wind speeds at that time. But the storm peeled bark off trees. This takes wind speeds over 200 miles (300 km) per hour. About 22,000 people died.

The Caribbean Islands are often in the path of hurricanes.

DID YOU KNOW?

The Great Hurricane of 1780 knocked down stone buildings, tossed cannons, and flipped over ships.

CHAPTER THREE

Can you prepare for a hurricane?

Yes! The National Weather Service (NWS) watches ocean storms. It warns people at least 36 hours before **landfall**. You have some time to get ready. Board up windows. Gather food, water, and first aid supplies. Listen to the news. **Evacuate** if necessary.

It's important to know your evacuation route before a hurricane.

Families should pack clothes, food, and water before a hurricane.

DID YOU KNOW?

You should never walk through flooded streets. Only 6 inches (15 centimeters) of moving water can knock you down.

What should you do if you stay home?

Stay in a small, safe space until the storm passes.

Keep away from windows. Go to a small inner room or closet. Move to the top floor if the house starts to flood. There may be calm weather as the eye passes over. This could last a couple of hours. Make sure the storm is over before going outdoors.

DID YOU KNOW?

These big storms make a huge mess. Pitch in and help your community clean up!

STAY CURIOUS!

ASK MORE QUESTIONS

Has there ever been a hurricane where I live?

When should you evacuate and stay put?

Try a BIG QUESTION: Where would my family go if we had to evacuate?

SEARCH FOR ANSWERS

Search the library catalog or the Internet.
A librarian, teacher, or parent can help you.

Using Keywords
Find the looking glass.

Keywords are the most important words in your question.

If you want to know about:

- hurricanes near you, type: HURRICANES IN (YOUR STATE)
- when to evacuate or stay put, type: STAY SAFE DURING A HURRICANE

LEARN MORE

FIND GOOD SOURCES

Here are some good, safe sources you can use in your research. Your librarian can help you find more.

Books

Hurricanes
by Marcia Abramson, 2024.

Hurricanes: The Worst in History
by Jenna Vale, 2025.

Internet Sites

NASA Space Place: How do hurricanes form?
https://spaceplace.nasa.gov/hurricanes/en/
NASA Space Place is an interactive site for kids. Explore topics about Earth and Space!

National Geographic Kids: Hurricanes
https://kids.nationalgeographic.com/science/article/hurricane
National Geographic Kids is an educational website for kids.

Every effort has been made to ensure that these websites are appropriate for children. However, because of the nature of the Internet, it's impossible to guarantee that these sites will remain active indefinitely or that their contents will not be altered.

SHARE AND TAKE ACTION

Make a list of items you might need during a storm emergency.

Pretend a hurricane has hit. Where in your house would you stay safe?

Make a hurricane in a jar! Ask an adult to help you find directions online.

GLOSSARY

damage The harm caused to something.

evacuate To leave a place and move somewhere safer.

eye The center of a hurricane.

landfall When a storm moves over land after being over water.

storm surge A big wave of water that gets pushed towards the shore by a strong storm.

tropical Having to do with warm and humid conditions.

INDEX

About the Author

Rachel Grack has been editing and writing children's books since 1999. She lives on a small ranch in the Arizona desert.